SO-AHF-827

STARTING A MARINE AQUARIUM

Starting a Marine Aquarium

CRAIG S. BARKER

Cover: A juvenile *Euxiphipops navarchus*. Photo by Earl Kennedy.

© Copyright 1972 by T.F.H. Publications, Inc. Ltd.

© Copyright 1980 by T.F.H. Publications, Inc. Ltd.

Distributed in the U.S. by T.F.H. Publications, Inc., PO Box 427, Neptune, NJ 07753; in England by T.F.H. (Gt. Britain) Ltd., 13 Nutley Lane, Reigate, Surrey; in Canada by Rolf C. Hagen Ltd., 3225 Sartelon Street, Montreal 382, Quebec; in Australia by Pet Imports Pty. Ltd., P.O. Box 149, Brookvale 2100, N.S.W. Australia; in South Africa by Valid Agencies, P.O. Box 51901, Randburg by T.F.H. Publications, Inc., Ltd, the British Crown Colony of Hong Kong.

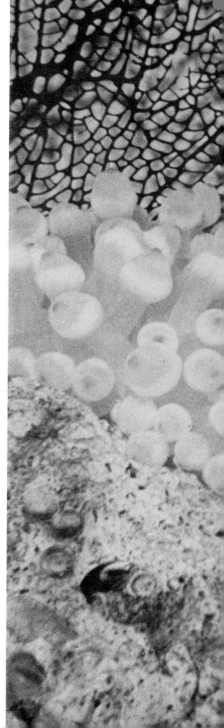

Amphiprion sebae.
Photo by Gerhard Budich.

Careful management of a marine aquarium will enable the aquarist to keep the beautiful coral reef fishes. Photo by Dr. Herbert R. Axelrod.

ABOUT THE AUTHOR

Craig Barker has been collecting, maintaining, and photographing marine tropicals since moving to South Florida in the mid nineteen-fifties. Collecting trips have taken him throughout South Florida, the Florida Keys, and the Bahama Islands. He has authored articles on marine aquariums and saltwater tropicals for several magazines.

While attending college, he operated an aquarium sales and servicing business on a part-time basis and ran a local aquarium shop. He received a Masters Degree in Business Administration from Florida Atlantic University and is currently working in the Technical Development Section of Aquatic Sciences, Inc., Boca Raton, Florida.

ABOUT THE ARRANGEMENT OF THIS BOOK: Page four and succeeding color pages show photographs of most of the individual fish and invertebrate species discussed in this book, plus other fishes and invertebrates that the marine aquarist will see from time to time. All photographs from page 40 on are arranged approximately in the order in which the subjects they portray are discussed in Chapter X (beginning page 63). For color photographs useful in the identification of hundreds of other marine fishes and for a more comprehensive view of the marine aquarium hobby, we direct the reader's attention to Exotic Marine Fishes, by Drs. Herbert R. Axelrod and C. W. Emmens. This looseleaf book is the standard hobby reference in the field; additions to it, covering new fishes, are made regularly.

TABLE OF CONTENTS

Opisthognathus aurifrons, pearly jawfish, family Opisthognathidae. This interesting species builds a tunnel-like burrow if provided with a sufficient depth of bottom covering in its aquarium. Photo by Craig Barker.

Taenionotus triacanthus, family Scorpaenidae. This poisonous fish is not seen often; like all other scorpaenids, it should be handled with care and is not a good fish for the beginning marine aquarist. Photo by Douglas Faulkner.

Balistoides niger, clown triggerfish, family Balistidae. This weirdly patterned triggerfish is a very expensive fish and infrequently seen in private collections, although it is a mainstay of public aquariums. This species previously was known as *Balistoides conspiculum* (with various spellings used for the specific name). Photo by Hans Peter.

INTRODUCTION

I am frequently asked how the keeping of a marine aquarium differs from the keeping of a freshwater aquarium. It is very difficult to answer this question in the short time that is usually allotted for the reply. In some ways they are very similar, but in other ways the difference is as plain as night and day. Briefly, the care required by a marine aquarium is more complicated than that demanded by a freshwater tank. Pollution and disease are likely to occur much more quickly and lethally in a marine aquarium than in a freshwater aquarium. There is no reason, however, why, if a hobbyist has successfully kept a freshwater aquarium, he cannot enjoy a successful marine aquarium with just a little more precise care.

One of the greatest features about the aquarium field in general, and marine aquariums in particular, is that the hobbyist can put as much, or as little, time and money into his hobby as he can afford. An individual can start with less than a day's pay invested in a glass bowl, air pump, food, filter, and a pair of seahorses. This can gradually increase until the hobbyist is curator over what seems to be a small oceanarium.

Tremendous progress has been made in the keeping of marine fish over the past decade. Much knowledge has been acquired and many new products have entered the market to facilitate the keeping of marine fish. This work is intended as a cursory guide to marine aquariums. Because of its brevity, only fundamentals will be covered, and it is recommended that the individual pursue more complete books on the subject.

The procedure outline herein for starting a marine aquarium is one that has been used successfully by many individuals for a number of years. There are many additions and modifications that may be made to the system recommended; however, it is the author's opinion that a great majority of successful home marine aquarists use subsand filters *and* outside filters (containing activated carbon) or a relatively slight modification thereof.

//

THE AQUARIUM: WHAT KIND AND HOW LARGE?

The first problem facing a potential marine hobbyist is the decision of purchasing an aquarium. What kind and how large should it be? The size will vary with the individual and his objectives. Assuming that one desires to keep a community aquarium, it is best to choose one with a capacity of between twenty-five and fifty gallons. It is too easy for the neophyte hobbyist to pollute tanks smaller than twenty-five gallons. Tanks larger than fifty gallons can prove expensive and burdensome, particularly to a beginning hobbyist, but get one if you can afford it.

Tanks smaller than twenty-five gallons may be satisfactory for marine aquariums, but the hobbyist will be limited in the number of fish he can put into it. If an individual gets carried away adding "just one more fish" to his freshwater aquarium, imagine what will happen the next time his dealer gets in a shipment of dazzling saltwater fish! Saltwater fish also have the potential to grow very quickly and will soon need more swimming space. An example of this was a French angelfish whose home was a ten-gallon aquarium. He then proceeded to outgrow both a twenty-gallon and a thirty-gallon aquarium, and finally was returned to the reef. Smaller tanks are good for displaying saltwater oddities such as moray eels, lionfish, seahorses, invertebrates, and many others.

The all-glass tank is the best for the marine aquarium. Since it contains no metal, there is no chance of corrosion and toxicity occurring such as with a metal aquarium. Today, as a matter of fact, all-glass aquariums are just about the only types manufactured and made available commercially—very few of the old-style metal-framed tanks are seen.

Some individuals have had success using homemade tanks of fiberglass, but unless they have used the proper resin and cured

Blennius nigriceps, the Carmine or Cardinal Blenny, family Blenniidae. Not many blennies are available to marine aquarists, and most of those seen are a good deal less colorful than the species shown. As most Mediterranean species, this fish prefers cooler water than most salt water tropicals. Photo by G. Marcuse.

Parupeneus pleurostigma, goatfish, family Mullidae. Although generally not highly favored by marine aquarists, the goatfishes make satisfactory fishes for beginners. Photo by Dr. Herbert R. Axelrod.

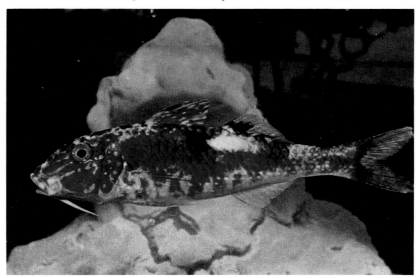

Lactoria cornutus, cowfish, family Ostraciontidae. A shy, interesting fish, so named because of its protruding "horns". Photo by G. Marcuse.

Apogon maculatus, cardinal fish, family Apogonidae. The cardinal-fishes are mostly small, inoffensive species that are fairly easy to maintain; usually inexpensive, and most make good species for maintenance by beginners. Noting their large mouth, they should be fed primarily live foods such as small guppies and shrimp. Photo by G. Marcuse.

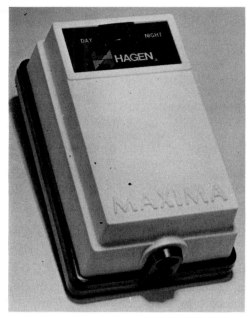

The selection of an air pump depends upon the number and type of pieces of air-powered equipment the pump will be required to operate. Today's vibrator pumps are very reliable and are very quiet as well; some (the "Maxima" pump shown is an example) are equipped with switches that convert the pump from day to night-time operation.

it considerably, the tank will render the aquarium water toxic and therefore useless in a few days. Plexiglas aquariums are fine for marine aquariums from a technical viewpoint, but not from an esthetic evaluation: they scratch easily and sometimes distort the view. They are also expensive. It is recommended that the beginning marine hobbyist stay with the all-glass aquarium. (The term "all-glass" is misleading to a certain extent, because all-glass tanks are not made exclusively of glass, of course; the glass pieces are joined by a silicone cement, and often the glass is framed in plastic.)

Soaps, detergents, and the like should not be used for cleaning the marine aquarium, as there is the possibility that they can get into the water and kill one's fish.

III

AQUARIUM FILTRATION: MECHANICAL AND BIOLOGICAL

Aquarium filtration can be broken down into two different types: mechanical and biological. Mechanical filtration consists of actually physically separating particles from the water in the aquarium. A variety of materials are commonly used for this purpose in aquarium management, including glass wool, dacron wool, and sand. Biological filtration takes place when aerobic bacteria oxidize organic waste materials that accumulate in the aquarium. This oxidation takes place on the upper layers of sand above a subsand filter and on the material that is used in external filters. To be successful, an aquarist should plan to make simultaneous use of both types of filtration.

Although there are many methods of filtering a marine aquarium (some very complex), it is difficult to imagine the beginning hobbyist having much success without using a subsand filter. It is true, filtering can be done by other means, but why stack the odds against yourself? A subsand filter is a piece of perforated plastic that lies on the bottom of the tank. Two tubes are attached to the plastic. Air is forced down through the smaller tube and allowed to rise to the surface in the larger tube. As the air rises it carries water with it to the surface. Water is drawn down through the sand (which was placed on top of the perforated plastic), and then through the plastic filter to replace the water forced to the surface.

The sand that was placed above the subsand filter acts first as a mechanical filter by trapping the various particles that were floating in the water, as this water is drawn down through the filter. Once the tank has been in operation for a few days, aerobic bacteria begin to accumulate on and around the tiny grains of sand. This concentration takes place primarily on the surface layer of sand. The number of aerobic bacteria drops drastically below the first few layers of sand. These bacteria oxidize the

Above: *Zebrasoma veliferum*, juvenile sailfin tang. Photo by Douglas Faulkner.
Below: *Acanthurus glaucopareius*, golden-rimmed surgeon.
Both species belong to the family Acanthuridae, surgeonfishes or tangs. Many tangs are highly colorful and interesting fishes, but they are usually very expensive. They need a lot of algae in their diet. Surgeonfishes are equipped with a spine near the tail. They use this spine as a weapon against other fishes. Photo by G. Marcuse.

Aeoliscus strigatus, one of the shrimpfishes, family Centriscidae. This bizarre fish is found in nature almost invariably in association with sea urchins. They are not particularly hardy, needing live adult brine shrimp for food. They should be maintained by themselves or with other harmless species such as seahorses and pipefishes. Photo by Klaus Paysan.

accumulations of organic waste that are drawn to the sand by the mechanical filtration properties of the subsand filter. Once the aerobic bacteria begin to oxidize the organic wastes, the subsand filter is acting as a biological filter as well as a mechanical filter.

The subsand filtering system will circulate, aerate, and filter the aquarium. It also helps to prevent pockets of gas from forming in the sand and other relatively stagnant areas from developing in the aquarium.

For best results some type of outside water-circulating filter should be used with a marine aquarium. This type of filtering device pulls the water out of the aquarium and into an outside container (usually hanging on the tank). Here the water passes through dacron or glass wool and activated carbon. Dacron is much more satisfactory than glass wool, and is used to remove the

Subsand filters circulate water through the bottom sand or gravel.

Power filters are often used for large marine aquaria.
Photo courtesy of
Eugene G. Danner Mfg. Inc.

Filters that use diatomaceous earth as their filtering agents are very efficient and can remove suspended dirt from the water very quickly.

Gymnothorax species, moray eel, family Muraenidae. Moray eels are one of the many oddities from the sea that can be kept by the home aquarist. Usually kept in a tank by themselves, with the aquarium having a weighted cover to prevent the eel's escape and eventual death. Photo by Douglas Faulkner.

Prionotus punctatus, sea robin, family Triglidae. Sea robins are curious additions to one's tank as they "walk" along the bottom. Occasionally they will spread their "wings" and glide. Live foods are preferred. Photo by U. Erich Friese.

Plectorhynchus chaetodonoides, clown sweetlips, family Plecto-rhynchidae. The clown sweetlips is a peaceful and hardy species from Singapore and the Philippine Islands. A fast grower, its attractive spots disappear as the fish matures. Photo by Earl Kennedy.

Calloplesiops altivelus, "comet," family Plesiopidae. This species is not seen very often and when available it ranks as one of the most expensive of marine tropicals. It is fairly hardy, although it does hide under coral a lot. Photo by S. Frank.

Ultraviolet sterilizers are used to kill pathogenic organisms before they have a chance to attack the fishes in the tank.

Canister-type outside power filters do a good filtering job and do not have to hang off the side of the tank.

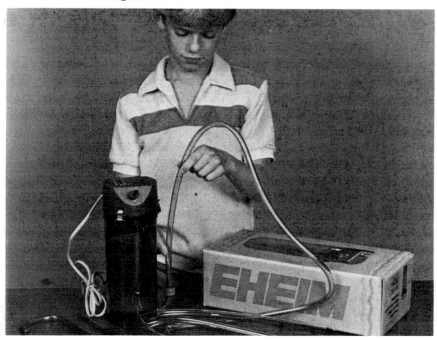

larger particles of foreign matter from the water. Since it is placed on top of the activated carbon, the dacron is relatively easy to change.

A good feature of the outside filter is that it permits the hobbyist to use activated carbon. Similar to charcoal, but much more absorbent, activated carbon removes from the water condensed gases and other pollutants which are too fine to be removed by the dacron. Activated carbon can make an aquarium, which has turned an "aged yellow," blue-white over night. Activated carbon should be rinsed with running fresh water for several hours if one is planning to use it in an already-established aquarium. New activated carbon can drastically change the pH of the water, causing fish to go into shock and die. To be safe it is a good idea to run the outside filter for a gradually increasing period of time the first few weeks. Start out with about fifteen minutes a day of running the filter and gradually increase the filtering period.

Aerobic bacteria will also accumulate on the dacron as water is circulated through the outside filter. They soon begin to oxidize organic wastes, and thus the outside filter begins to act as a biological filter as well as a mechanical filter.

Outside filters can be classified into two main types: those that use an electric motor to pump the water and those that use the air-lift principle similar to that employed in a subsand filter. Generally speaking, the motor-driven type pumps more water more often than the air-lift type.

Although not recommended for the beginning marine hobbyist, there are other types of filtration systems in use by hobbyists. One type uses only aeration and live coral, while another makes use of algae. The reader is referred to books and periodicals with more extensive information concerning other systems.

Canthigaster solandri, sharp-nosed puffer, family Canthigasteridae. The sharp-nosed puffers for the most part are hardy and colorful. An amusing fish to watch as he "rolls" his eyes inspecting the aquarium. Photo by Klaus Paysan.

Pervagor species, filefish, family Monacanthidae. Filefishes are hardy, although they have a tendency to fight among themselves. Photo by U. Erich Friese.

Platax species, batfish, family Platacidae. Young batfishes are often available at prices within the reach of most aquarists, but mature specimens are expensive. Specimens grow fast however, and hobbyists may soon find themselves buying a larger aquarium for their favorite pet. Photo by Douglas Faulkner.

Zanclus canescens, Moorish idol, family Zanclidae. Expensive and delicate, the Moorish idol is not for beginners. Most of the difficulty involved in keeping this species stems from the fact that it feeds almost exclusively on live coral polyps—a difficult diet to provide. Photo by Douglas Faulkner.

IV

DECORATING THE MARINE AQUARIUM

When decorating the marine aquarium, more than just esthetic evaluations should be taken into consideration. It is important to remember that whatever one places in the aquarium can affect the chemistry of the water and the psychology of its inhabitants. With very few exceptions, most of the creatures which you place in your aquarium will have been very shortly removed from their natural environment—the ocean. In order to make them feel at home it is wise for the hobbyist to make the fish's new home as natural as possible.

Aquarium decorations can be useful as well as decorative. Sea horses require something to hold on to with their tails. Photo courtesy of N.Y.Z.S.

Black coral is related to the sea fan and often used as a decoration for marine tanks. Photo by Dr. Herbert R. Axelrod.

In choosing sand for the aquarium, one must find sand that will not be so fine as to clog the subsand filter, yet not so coarse as to harbor fairly large uneaten particles of food or cause injury to the fish. For best results use regular-grain silica sand in the aquarium. Some hobbyists use beach sand for their aquariums, but finding beach sand with the proper consistency can be a difficult problem. Also beach sand can contain dangerous foreign matter that is difficult to remove. If one desires to obtain a beach-like effect in his aquarium, small particles of crushed and shattered sea shells can be sprinkled on top of the silica. No matter what type sand one uses, be sure it is washed well before placing it in the aquarium.

Coral is a natural addition to a marine aquarium. Although live coral is being kept by advanced hobbyists, it is best omitted from a beginner's aquarium. Coral that has been purchased from gift shops and other stores can be used in a marine aquarium *provided it is properly prepared*. Since store-bought coral has already been partially cured, it is necessary only to boil the coral. Do not use dyed coral in tanks unless this dyeing was done specifically for salt-water aquariums. To be safe only buy from your petshop.

Juvenile trunkfishes make excellent aquarium fishes. These *Ostracion cubicus* are less than 1½″ long. Photo by Robert P. L. Straughan.

Plotosus anguillaris, salt water catfish, family Plotosidae. Extreme care should be taken when handling this species as its dorsal and pectoral fins can be toxic to humans. The young are more highly colored than the adults. It is a hardy eater. Photo by Klaus Paysan.

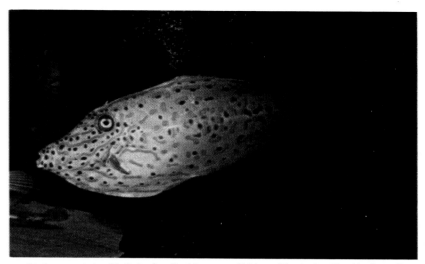

Alutera scripta, filefish, family Monacanthidae. Photo by Dr. Herbert R. Axelrod.

Antennarius hispidus, anglerfish, family Antennariidae. This sluggish but voracious master of camouflage should not be kept with any other fish small enough to swallow, the same applying to the other angler-fishes. Photo by H. Hansen, Aquarium Berlin.

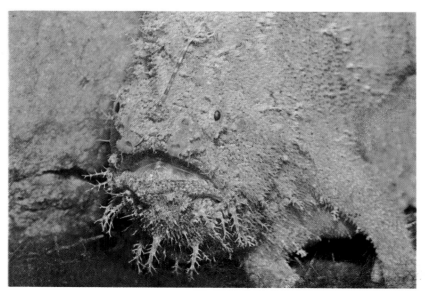

Coral that has been collected from the ocean should be soaked in a strong solution of bleach. This will kill the polyps and other inhabitants that the piece of coral might contain. If this is not done, these inhabitants would probably soon die and pollute the tank. After soaking the coral for 5–10 days, one should rinse it well to remove the chlorine and any impurities, and then soak the coral in fresh water for at least a week. If the coral and water in which it has been soaking are free of odor from chlorine or decaying matter, the coral is safe to use in the aquarium. If coral is not free from odor and decaying matter, repeat the cleansing procedure until it is.

In selecting the types of coral for your aquarium, remember that the fish will make the coral their home. It offers them a place to hide from the prying eyes of humans. Pieces of coral such as Pacific finger coral and Pacific lettuce coral are usually too dense to offer specimens shelter, and will only serve to collect uneaten food particles. Atlantic lettuce coral, staghorn coral, and hollowed-out pieces of brain coral make practical additions to the aquarium. Red pipe organ coral makes a colorful addition to the tank.

Red Coral is attractive and can be shaped easily. However, it is also difficult to clean. Photo by Douglas Faulkner.

These two examples of coral are a small sample of the many types suitable for the marine aquaria. Photos by Dr. Herbert R. Axelrod.

Epinephelus flavocoeruleus, blue and yellow reef-cod (grouper), family Serranidae. Groupers are not very popular among marine hobbyists, mostly because they grow too large for keeping in any but the largest of tanks. They usually lose their attractive juvenile markings and are strictly predaceous fishes that will try to engulf anything small enough to swallow. Photo by H. Hansen, Aquarium Berlin.

Chromileptis altivelis, polka dot grouper, family Serranidae. This is one of the best groupers for maintenance by marine aquarists, as it is not a hider and keeps its attractive markings throughout its life. Photo by H. Hansen, Aquarium Berlin.

Gobiosoma oceanops, neon goby, family Gobiidae. The neon goby is one of the few gobies available, but it is one of the most popular of all marine fishes, being inexpensive and hardy. A measure of the fish's capacity to adapt to aquarium life is that it has spawned in home marine aquaria many times, although no one has yet succeeded in raising the fry to maturity. The neon goby is a parasite-picker, removing parasites from its tankmates in much the same fashion as the "cleaner" wrasses. Photo by Douglas Faulkner.

Scarus species, parrotfish, family Scaridae (also known as family Callyodontidae). Some of the parrotfishes, which are closely related to the wrasses, are very colorful, but they are in the main very expensive. Parrotfishes don't do particularly well in marine aquariums primarily due to diet deficiencies. On the reef they eat plant life and actually bite off bits of live coral, chewing it like a mouthful of stones. Photo by G. Marcuse.

One procedure followed by some hobbyists is to remove a piece of coral the minute it becomes spotted with algae. The piece is bleached and then returned to the tank. If properly done, the bleaching process will not harm the fish, but the hobbyist has killed an important source of snacks for his fish—the algae. In such a sterile, pale environment many fish quickly suffer from a fading of their colors.

All things considered, sea shells should be left out of the marine aquarium. No matter how carefully cleaned, there always seem to be particles of the original owner left in the cone of the shell. These, of course, can pollute the water. Since water cannot circulate through a perfectly intact shell, the water in the shell soon goes bad and then the fish will not swim into it. Best shells for the marine aquarium are those that have been badly damaged or broken, exposing much of the interior. This allows for a freer flow of water with no pollution likely, and small fish and invertebrates take delight in swimming through such a shell.

Live plants are being kept by more advanced hobbyists, but these plants can die quickly and pollute the tank, and should be omitted from the novice's marine aquarium. Some plastic plants can be used in the marine aquarium provided no parts are made of metal. Some, however, have a metal stem which, although covered with plastic, sooner or later manages to come in contact with the salt water. Since most plastic plants are fashioned after freshwater species, why bother to put them in a saltwater aquarium? There are, however, plastic corals and plastic sea fans which are perfectly acceptable.

V

WATER FOR THE MARINE AQUARIUM

The hobbyist is now ready to procure the water for his marine aquarium. He can choose either natural sea water or an artificial salt mix. Since most hobbyists are not located near the ocean, artificial salts have enjoyed increased popularity in recent years. While expensive and not too consistent in quality a decade ago, today there are many varieties available at a moderate cost which are excellent for a marine aquarium. Many South Florida hobbyists find it easier to use synthetic mixes than to haul water all the way from the ocean. Although there are several formulas available for making one's own salt water, the beginner will find it easier, cheaper, and probably much more successful to use a commercially prepared mix.

If the hobbyist decides to collect his own water from the sea, he should obtain it from a location that is free from pollution—both man-made and natural. The water should be clear, clean, and odorless. If the water contains small particles of foreign matter, such as seaweed, it should be filtered or strained before placing it in the aquarium. Dacron can be used for this purpose. Water should always be collected and transported in a nontoxic (non-metal) container. Plastic buckets and bags are ideal for this task.

A hydrometer is essential to determine the specific gravity of the water. The hydrometer should read around 1.025. This figure relates to the amount of salt in the water. Since the salt in the water does not evaporate, it is necessary to add only fresh water to replace the volume lost through evaporation. If more salt water were added, it would increase the salt content of the water and eventually be damaging to the fish's health.

Many hobbyists maintain the salinity of their marine aquarium by placing a mark on the aquarium glass at the water level. They maintain a constant salinity by simply filling the tank with fresh water to the mark when the water has evaporated. This method is fairly accurate only if the hobbyist remembers to calculate for the water displacement caused by transferring different size pieces of

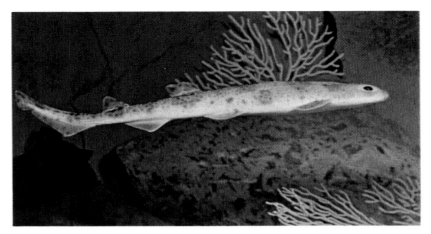

Sharks and other elasmobranchs are not often seen in marine aquaria but very small specimens make interesting objects for observation if maintained in tanks large enough to house them comfortably. Shown is a young European dogfish *(Scyliorhinus canicula)* of the catshark family, Scyliorhinidae. Photo by Klaus Paysan.

Rhinomuraena amboinensis, ribbon eels, family Muraenidae. Although these eels belong to the same family as the moray eels, they are far less vicious and easier to keep. Occasionally offered for sale at high prices, they are much in demand by experienced salt water hobbyists. Photo by K. H. Choo.

This clingfish from the Mediterranean Sea is so named because the pelvic fins are modified into a sucking disk that enables it to cling to the surface of plants or rocks. Photo by H. Hansen, Aquarium Berlin.

Some snappers, as this *Lutjanis sanguineus*, are brightly colored as juveniles. Unfortunately, they grow large quickly and tend to become sombre-colored. Photo by H. Hansen, Aquarium Berlin.

A hydrometer is necessary to determine the specific gravity of the water in the tank. The hydrometer shown is one of the newer types, easier to read than the older floating types.

Today's products for making up artificial salt water are in general excellent; these products make it possible for every aquarist, even those living far from the ocean, to enjoy the marine aquarium hobby.

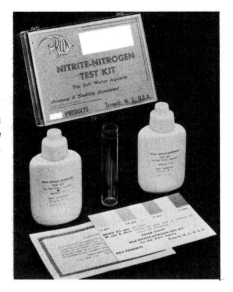

Additional test kits for analyzing aquarium water chemistry are available.

coral from one tank to another and to allow for water removed for transferring specimens.

There are several sizes of hydrometers available to the hobbyist. Generally speaking, the hobbyist should acquire the largest size possible. The smaller hydrometers, five and six inches, are often inaccurate, and could cause trouble if the hobbyist tries to adjust to the reading of a faulty hydrometer. Some hydrometers also contain thermometers.

The pH of the water refers to its measure of alkalinity or acidity, and should be around 8.2. While there are several types of pH measuring kits on the market, there is some question as to how accurate they are in reality. In a properly maintained marine aquarium, pH will gradually decrease. It is not advisable to add chemicals whenever the pH reads a slight variance from 8.2.

pH consideration is most important when transferring fish from one body of water to another. Chances are that the pH of the two waters are different. Marine fish can stand a gradual change in the pH, but sudden transfer can put them into shock and often results in their death. To avoid this shock, it is important to gradually acclimate the fish to the water into which it is going. This can be done by placing the fish in a separate container with its old water,

Pomacanthus paru, French angelfish (Juvenile): Photo by Dr. Herbert R. Axelrod.

Holacanthus ciliaris, queen angelfish: Photo by Dr. Herbert R. Axelrod.

Pomacanthus arcuatus, black angelfish (Adult): Photo by Dr. John E. Randall.

Parasites, diseases, or lack of proper diet can lead to an emaciated
condition and eventually death in your fishes. Photo by G. Marcuse.

and mixing gradually by pouring the new water into the container.
To be safe, this process should be performed at half-hour intervals
lasting for several hours. Losing a fish from pH shock is a needless
loss, caused by neglect and carelessness.

The water temperature should be between 72 and 80 degrees
and, as with pH, sudden changes in this factor should be avoided.
Since the fish will probably come from the coral reefs where
oxygen content is high, plenty of aeration should be provided for
the aquarium. Aeration serves to circulate the water, allowing
oxygen to enter the water and carbon dioxide to escape. With a
marine aquarium it is wise to have an extra air pump available
should the main pump fail to function.

VI

FEEDING MARINE FISHES

It is important that one's marine tropicals receive both the proper amount and types of food in their diet. The food requirements vary from fish to fish, and each species' needs should be considered when planning their meals. Fish with rather large mouths such as squirrel fish, cardinal fish, snappers, and groupers are mostly carnivorous and, therefore, require more meat and fish in their diet than angelfish which are fond of greens. It should be remembered that fish with a small mouth have a difficult time swallowing large chunks of food and fish with big mouths enjoy large portions. In other words, tailor the meals to your individual specimens.

Cut-up pieces of shrimp, scallops, lobster, and fish are enjoyed by most species. Greens should be provided in the form of lettuce and algae. Most commercially prepared flake mixes contain some dried greens, and certain brands are composed entirely of greens. Algae that are allowed to grow in the aquarium make an excellent source of snacks for one's fish. The freeze-dried foods offer a selection of foods that were previously hard to obtain and messy when available. The menu includes daphnia, brine shrimp, fairy shrimp, tubifex worms, and others.

Frozen brine shrimp is an excellent contribution to the fish's diet provided that the shrimp is of a good quality. The hobbyist should be able to distinguish the body of the shrimp when the mixture is thawed in water. If the shrimp is not whole or is broken into pieces, the food content and value is questionable. Live brine shrimp is relished by one's marines, and has the added advantage of staying alive in the aquarium until consumed.

Brine shrimp, freeze dried, frozen or live, should not be allowed to become the sole diet of one's marines. Experiments with angelfish have shown that specimens fed exclusively on brine shrimp, although eating their fill daily, gradually lose their color and waste away. The importance of greens in the diet of such species cannot be overstated.

Holacanthus arcuatus, Hawaiian banded angelfish: Photo by Dr. Herbert R. Axelrod.

Centropyge vroliki, pearl-scaled angelfish: Photo by U. Erich Friese.

Centropyge flavissimus, lemon peel: Photo by Klaus Paysan.

Centropyge bispinosus, coral beauty: Photo by U. Erich Friese.

Brine shrimp is one of the staples of the marine diet. All stages, from newly hatched to adult, are accepted. Photo of adult brine shrimp by Dr. Herbert R. Axelrod.

It is easy to pollute a marine aquarium, particularly if one is feeding cut-up pieces of fish, lobster, etcetera. Even brine shrimp can be guilty of pollution. When feeding these foods it is best to add the food to the tank in amounts that are readily consumed by the fish. Uneaten pieces of food can cloud an aquarium overnight.

Since fish are constantly nibbling in the ocean, it is recommended that they be fed more than once a day in the aquarium. One procedure consists of feeding a high-quality flake food in the morning, and during the afternoon or evening feeding brine shrimp or cut-up fish.

VII

DISEASES

Sometime after your marine aquarium has been set up and operating you might notice that your fish are acting in a peculiar manner. Perhaps their appetite has waned, they are scratching themselves on the coral and sand, or perhaps they are just swimming at the surface of the water apparently gasping for air. Such occurrences are usually indicators of disease in the tank.

Most disease in a marine aquarium is in the form of various parasites. These parasites can be introduced into the aquarium with new fish and food, or can be transferred from one tank to another by a careless hobbyist. Parasites are a common problem among saltwater tropicals and are characterized by small spots in the body of the fish. Scratching is a symptom of this disease.

There are now several commercial remedies on the market which can control many parasitic diseases. They usually contain either copper sulfate or sulfathiazole sodium, or a mixture of the two. Medication with copper sulfate and citric acid has been found by many to be the most successful.

Most medication can be harmful to your fish if used in excessive amounts; therefore, instructions on the container should be carefully followed. Avoid mixing various remedies. Most invertebrates are harmed by medication, and a tank containing them should not be treated. The fish should be removed to a separate tank. Invertebrates should not be put into tanks which have been treated with medication previously, even at a much earlier date. Shrimp seem to be especially susceptible to this type of poisoning.

Sometimes a fish's fins begin to look ragged. This can be caused by the nipping of his fins by his tankmates or a bacterial infection called fin rot. Fin-nipping usually results in a case of fin rot. This can be cured by taking the fish from the aquarium and gently painting the infected area with merthiolate or mercurochrome. Care should be taken not to get any of these drugs in the fish's gills. The fins will gradually grow back provided the fish is well fed and not placed with the same aggressors again.

Centropyge argi, pygmy angelfish: Photo by Karl Probst.

Pomacanthus maculosus, blue-moon angelfish: Photo by U. Erich Friese.

Pomacanthus semicirculatus, Koran angelfish (Juvenile): Photo by Douglas Faulkner.

Pomacanthus imperator, imperial angelfish: Photo by H. Hansen, Aquarium Berlin.

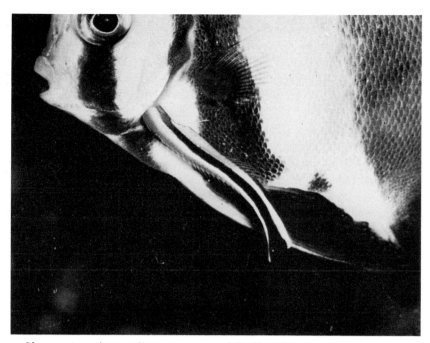

Many external parasites are removed by the cleaner wrasses, genus *Labroides*. Photo by Müller—Schmida.

Larger external parasites are sometimes encountered on marine fish. These can be removed with tweezers if utmost care is taken not to injure the fish. Since their parasites can be deeply attached to the host, it may be necessary to first kill the parasite and remove him piece by piece.

VIII

SETTING UP A MARINE AQUARIUM

When planning a marine aquarium it is best to allow time for the tank, once set up, to filter and operate for two or three weeks before adding one's valuable specimens. This "break-in" period, as it is often referred to, offers three main advantages. First of all, it gives one the opportunity to be sure that the mechanics of the aquarium system are working properly. Secondly, it allows the activated carbon time to filter the water, and avoids the possibility of any pH shock from this source. Thirdly, it allows the ammonia, nitrite, and nitrate levels of the aquarium to go through a cycle which results in these levels eventually being at an amount tolerable to marine species.

As soon as the aquarium is set up it begins to undergo chemical changes. Fish are added. They are fed. Not all of the food is consumed by the fishes, and it drops to the bottom of the aquarium. Here it is decomposed by aerobic bacteria. The feces, or excretory products, from the fishes and other living organisms in the tank also reach the bottom and the aerobic bacteria. Both the uneaten food and feces are high in nitrogen content, which appears as ammonia (NH_4). Through bacterial oxidation it becomes nitrite (NO_2), and finally nitrate (NO_3). During the "breaking-in" stage the levels of ammonia and nitrite reach amounts that are toxic to certain species. The amounts of ammonia and nitrites that a particular fish can tolerate vary from species to species. Species that can tolerate larger amounts of ammonia and nitrites are put in a newly set-up aquarium, and are used as "break-in" species until the aquarium has completed the ammonia, nitrite, and nitrate cycles. These fish are then removed, and the less hardy but more colorful reef species are added. See Chapter IX on Maintaining A Marine Aquarium for more information on ammonia, nitrites, and nitrates.

The tank should be placed in a location that is free from draft and excessive sunlight. The draft can cause sudden chills and

Two *Chaetodon fasciatus* and four surgeonfishes (family Acanthuridae) browse among coral formations in their Red Sea home waters. Photo by L. Sillner.

Chaetodon striatus, banded butterflyfish: Photo by Douglas Faulkner.

Chaetodon multicinctus, pebbled butterflyfish: Photo by Douglas Faulkner.

Synthetic salt water can be made from any of several commercial salt mixes.

Filter materials especially designed for marine aquaria are now present on the market.

result in a diseased tank. The sunlight can warm the tank too much in the summer. Otherwise, sunlight will help algae grow in the aquarium, thus providing the fish with a source of snacks. The tanks should not be placed in a room or location where the fish will be subject to sudden shocks caused by lights being turned on and off. This can cause them to go into shock and dash around the aquarium, running into anything in their path.

After the tank has been washed thoroughly, it is time to add the water. If synthetic salts are used, fill the tank with fresh water first and then add salts until a salinity of 1.025 is achieved. Above all, read and follow the directions on the package of artificial salts. After this has been done, or if you are using natural sea water, the subsand filter can be added. The plastic sheet should be tilted as it is placed in the tank to prevent any air pockets from forming under the plastic and impeding filtration. The gravel is added next, with one to two inches a satisfactory depth, depending upon the type of fish one adds. Many species will rearrange the sand or gravel to their own liking, no matter how artistic your set-up. The royal gramma is particularly fond of excavating a cave for himself under a rock, piece of coral, or *Tridacna* shell.

The coral and rocks can now be placed in the tank. These should be arranged in such a manner as to provide shelter for the fish and yet be attractive to the viewer. It is essential, however, that the fish have some place to hide from the aquarium light should it be too strong for them.

When selecting fish it is best to acquire almost a tankful at one time. Once fish have been introduced and settled in an aquarium they become hostile to most intruders. Types of fish that might have been added originally might not be successfully added later because of this factor. When adding fish to the aquarium be sure to acclimate them as outlined earlier.

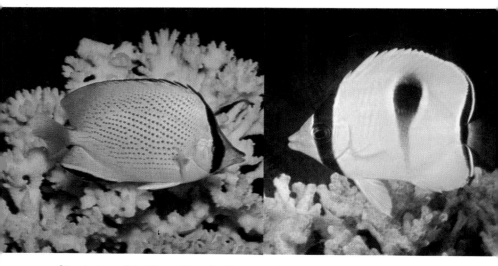

Chaetodon citrinellus, citron butterflyfish: Photo by Douglas Faulkner.

Chaetodon unimaculatus, tear-drop
butterflyfish: Photo by Douglas
Faulkner.

Chaetodon lunula, raccoon butterflyfish: Photo by Douglas Faulkner.

Chaetodon fremblii, blue-striped
butterflyfish: Photo by Douglas
Faulkner.

Chaetodon miliaris, milletseed butterflyfish: Photo by Douglas Faulkner.

Chaetodon mesoleucos, Red Sea butterflyfish: Photo by G. Marcuse.

IX

MAINTAINING A MARINE AQUARIUM

As mentioned in the Introduction, pollution and disease occur much more quickly and lethally in a marine aquarium than in a freshwater aquarium. This means that the hobbyist must be sure to check his aquarium on a regular basis, and at least once a day. These checks only take a few minutes, but the hobbyist must be sure that the aquarium is functioning properly mechanically, and that the tank's inhabitants are not exhibiting any signs of stress from either parasites or pollution.

If the hobbyist's home lacks central heating and air conditioning, the temperature of the water should also be monitored on a daily basis. Provided that the tank has been placed in a satisfactory location, and a high quality heater installed, temperature should not be too much of a problem.

After the aquarium has been "broken-in" the ammonia and nitrite amounts in the aquarium water remain fairly constant at acceptable levels. It is the level of nitrates that slowly continues to rise. Ammonia and nitrites are known to be most potentially toxic to marine species. Nitrates have been shown to interfere with respiration in octopuses, but to date similar effects have not been demonstrated with fishes. However, most hobbyists prefer not to take a chance with the lives of their valuable species.

The rising level of nitrates in the aquarium and other problems can be alleviated through partial changes of water. These water changes will also replace the various trace elements in the water which may have been used up by the tank's inhabitants. The pH of the water in a marine aquarium gradually decreases. The various buffers which are used to counteract this reduction only reduce the speed of this decline.

How often and how much of the water in a marine aquarium should be changed during these periodic water changes? The answer to this question varies from hobbyist to hobbyist. The variety of answers that one receives to this question is because the theoretically correct answer, if one could indeed establish the most desirable parameters, varies from aquarium to aquarium. The rise of nitrates, nitrites, ammonia, etc. varies with the size of the aquarium, the number of fish in the tank, the kind and amount of food that is fed the fish, and other variables. These variables must all be taken into account when trying to establish a formula for computing the point at which the periodic water changes should occur. Generally speaking, a one-third water change every three months produces satisfactory results. Some hobbyists prefer to change one-half the water every six months. Smaller, but more frequent water changes are to be preferred over larger, less frequent changes. First of all, the water in the aquarium is not given as much time to change substantially and secondly, the net effect of the change will not be as great, nor therefore as likely to cause the tank's inhabitants to experience stress or shock.

Some marine aquarists maintain that you need never change the water even partially, except when you completely clean out the aquarium. This statement is often made because the aquarist has had some species live for over a year in the aquarium, while the hobbyist has only replaced the water that has evaporated. The problem developing in this situation is that these specimens have become adjusted to the unusual water conditions which result from lengthy recirculation and reuse of the water. This change in water condition did not harm the fish while it was occurring as the change was gradual. It is extremely difficult to transfer specimens that have been adjusted to these unusual water conditions. The result is often death for one's long-lived specimens even when the acclimation period is gradual and carefully executed. What good are long-lived specimens if one cannot transfer them to another tank in case of emergency?

Growths of algae help to reduce the level of nitrates in the aquarium by utilizing it in their daily biological functions. Therefore a high growth of algae will reduce the rate at which the nitrates accumulate. Some marine aquarists help to reduce the level of nitrates through the use of autotrophic filters. These filters pass the water in the aquarium over or through large amounts of plant life in the hope that the plants will condition the water.

The beginning marine aquarist should simply make periodic changes of water until he has experienced sufficient success,

Chaetodon quadrimaculatus, 4-spot butterflyfish: Photo by Dr. Herbert R. Axelrod.

Chaetodon kleinii, Klein's butterflyfish: Photo by H. Hansen, Aquarium Berlin.

Chelmon rostratus, copper band long-nose: Photo by G. Marcuse.

Forcipiger flavissimus, long-nosed butterflyfish: Photo by Dr. Herbert R. Axelrod.

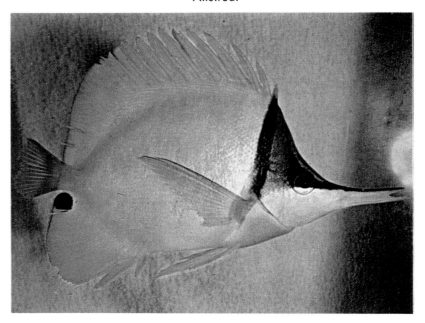

before he attempts to make use of autotrophic filtration.

In addition to the above practices, the marine hobbyists should also keep adequate records of his aquarium so that he will experience more success with his aquarium the next time around. Such factors as what was fed, the salinity of the water, the amount of light that the tank received, and other variables should also be observed and recorded so that the hobbyist will have some records as to the effect that these variables had on his marine aquarium. The hobbyist is warned, however, against over-simplifying the results of his hobby. These notes should only serve as guidelines and not the final word as to caring for a marine aquarium.

Pomacanthus annularis from the Indian Ocean has two different color patterns. This adult used to have vertical pale blue and white stripes. Photo by Laurence E. Perkins.

X

FISHES FOR A HOME AQUARIUM
Butterflyfishes and Angelfishes (Family— Chaetodontidae)

The angelfishes and butterflyfishes (family Chaetodontidae) are a frequently kept family of saltwater aquarium fish. This family has representatives in tropical waters throughout the world, and many of them make excellent additions to the marine aquarium. Angelfishes (subfamily Pomacanthinae) can be distinguished from the butterflyfishes (subfamily Chaetodontinae) by the spine located on their gill covers.

Most of the angelfishes are colored differently during the juvenile stage from what they are in the adult stage. Angelfishes are usually quarrelsome with other members of their subfamily and therefore should be kept one to an aquarium. It is sometimes possible to keep more than one in an aquarium provided there is approximately an inch difference in their size, the aquarium is fairly large (over twenty-five gallons), and the fish are introduced into the aquarium at the same time. An angelfish will tend to become the "boss" in his aquarium, and care should be taken to see that the specimens that share his home will bend to his will.

Angelfish are hardy eaters once acclimated to the aquarium, although Atlantic species are better eaters than many Pacific species. Angelfishes like brine shrimp (baby or adult, depending on the fish's size), cut-up shrimp, fish, scallops, and a high quality dry food. It is very important that they receive some greens in their diet if they are to survive longer than a few months. This can be in the form of lettuce, algae, or dry food. Angelfishes can stuff their stomachs every day on brine shrimp but still suffer a loss of color and eventually waste away without some greens in their diet.

Favorites from the Caribbean area include the French angelfish (*Pomacanthus paru*) and the black angelfish (*P. arcuatus*). The young of these species are black with yellow vertical stripes. The

Heniochus acuminatus, bannerfish: Photo by Klaus Paysan.

juvenile French angelfish's tail has a rounded yellow band, while the rear band of the black angelfish is transparent and appears to be cut off straight. The queen angelfish (*Holacanthus ciliaris*) and blue angelfish (*H. bermudensis*) are also similar to each other when young. The young queen angelfish is usually orange in areas where the young blue angelfish is yellow. Differentiating between these two species is further complicated by hybridization of the two species, which results in many slightly different color patterns. Some specimens, which were the result of this hybridization, were once thought to be a separate species and named the Townsend angelfish.

The rock beauty (*Holacanthus tricolor*) is an angelfish that lives in the waters near the edge of the Gulf Stream off Florida's East Coast and throughout the coral reefs of the Caribbean. The large black area on its sides grows from a tiny spot, surrounded by a light blue circle, when it is very young to a size in adulthood that covers almost two-thirds of the fish's body. The pygmy angelfish (*Centropyge argi*) grows to around a maximum of five inches, contrasted with the usual one or two-foot length of the other angelfish. This is a deep-water fish from the Bahamas, usually found in over forty feet of water. The pygmy angelfish was unknown until the late 1950's when it was discovered by tropical fish collectors in waters off Bimini in the Bahamas.

Favorite Pacific angelfish include two members of the same genus as the pygmy angelfish, the lemon peel (*Centropyge flavissimus*) and the Potter's angelfish (*C. potteri*). The imperial angelfish (*Pomacanthus imperator*) and the Koran angelfish (*P. semicirculatus*) both grow through different color stages while transforming from the juvenile to adult stage. Many other species of angelfish are available from the Pacific area, but the beginning hobbyist should stick with species that are known to be hardy rather than spend a lot of money on a very rare fish.

While not as colorful or flashy as the angelfishes, the butterflyfishes nevertheless are an interesting addition to one's marine aquarium. The butterflyfishes are more delicate in coloration and petite in manners than the angelfishes. Unlike the angelfishes, the juveniles of the butterflyfishes have patterns that closely resemble the adults. They also are not as quarrelsome as angelfishes and more than one member of the same species may be kept in the

Two of the anemonefishes generally sold under the name "tomato clownfish." Above, *Amphiprion ephippium:* Photo by Klaus Paysan; below, *Amphiprion melanopus:* Photo by Dr. Gerald R. Allen.

One of the "skunk" clowns, *Amphiprion sandaracinos* from the Philippines: Photo by Dr. Herbert R. Axelrod.

Clown anemonefish, generally known in the aquarium trade as *Amphiprion percula*, although a recent revision of the anemonefishes by Dr. Gerald F. Allen identifies this fish as *Amphiprion ocellaris*, with *A. percula* being a valid but distinct species. Photo by Douglas Faulkner.

The reef corals provide food as well as protection for many of the colorful fishes. Photo by Dr. W. Klausewitz.

same aquarium. Several species may also be mixed. Western Atlantic Ocean butterflyfishes are usually full-grown between four and six inches as compared with several feet in length for most angelfishes. Butterflyfishes swim in pairs or small schools when mature and wander about the reefs, while angelfishes pick out a certain area and make it their home. With these and other characteristic differences, there is some disagreement as to whether or not they belong in the same family—or are even closely related.

The foureye butterflyfish (*Chaetodon capistratus*), the banded butterflyfish (*C. striatus*), and the spotfin butterflyfish (*C. ocellatus*) can be grouped together as far as eating habits are concerned. They are fussy eaters and often waste away from starvation in captivity. On the reef these species nibble on tentacles of living corals and tubeworms. The best bet for keeping these and other fussy butterflyfishes in captivity is to obtain them fairly small, around an inch, as at this size they will accept baby brine shrimp, and may be gradually weaned to other foods as they grow older. Tubifex and white worms are sometimes taken by these finicky eaters. The spotfin butterflyfish is sometimes referred to as the common butterflyfish but, since this species is not common, the name spotfin butterflyfish is gaining a wider popularity.

The reef, painted, or least butterflyfish *(Chaetodon sedentarius)* is the hardiest of the butterflyfishes. It quickly adapts to life in captivity and is an eager eater. Two Pacific butterflyfish *(Chaetodon auriga* and *Chaetodon lunula)* are also hardy eaters and a good investment.

The Atlantic long-nosed butterflyfish is a deep-water specimen from the Caribbean. While not as hardy as the reef butterflyfish, it still does very well in the marine aquarium. The Atlantic long-nosed butterflyfish should not be confused with two Pacific species also known for their protruding snouts. *Forcipiger longirostris* is a Hawaiian species, while *Chelmon rostratus* is native to the Philippines and other Pacific areas. The snout of these two species is much longer than the Atlantic variety. In all three species the elongated snout is used for poking between pieces of coral searching for food.

Heniochus acuminatus, sometimes referred to as the long-finned butterflyfish or bannerfish, is a striking addition to the marine aquarium. Differing experiences are reported with this fish. Some hobbyists claim it is extremely easy to maintain, while others claim it is as difficult as a moorish idol to keep alive. When purchasing a *Heniochus*, as with any butterflyfish, it is best to purchase a specimen that is healthy and eating in your dealer's aquarium.

Damselfishes (Family—Pomacentridae)

The damselfish family (Pomacentridae) contains a wide variety of popular marine aquarium fish. This family is usually small in size, under six inches, and is strongly territorial in nature. One characteristic of this family is that these species have only one nostril on each side of the nose, while most fish have two nostrils on each side. Included in this family are such species as anemone-fish, three-spot *Dascyllus*, beau gregory, sergeant major, and blue reef fish.

The anemonefish (genus *Amphiprion*) includes around a dozen little fish sometimes referred to as clownfishes. These species live in and around the tentacles of sea anemones, generally *Discosoma*

Pomacentrus coeruleus, blue demoiselle: Photo by Douglas Faulkner.

Abudefduf saxatilis, sergeant major: Photo by Dr. Herbert R. Axelrod.

Pomacentrus leucostictus, beau gregory: Photo by Dr. Herbert R. Axelrod.

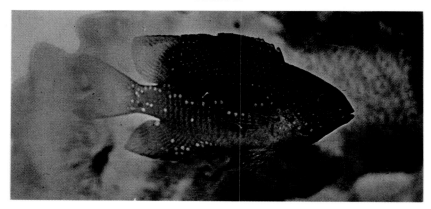

Dascyllus aruanus, black and white damselfish.

Dascyllus trimaculatus, three-spot *Dascyllus* or three-spot damsel-fish.

Photos by Dr. Herbert R. Axelrod.

and *Stoichactis*. Normally, contact with the tentacles of a sea anemone would mean death for a fish, but the anemonefish secretes a mucus which protects them from the stinging nematocysts of the sea anemone.

The anemonefish and sea anemone are examples of symbiosis in that both species benefit from the relationship (mutualism). The anemonefish is provided shelter and protection from predators, for which he in return brings bits of food for the anemone to devour. The constant swimming of these fish around the tentacles is also likely to help circulate water around the anemone. This could be construed as feeding itself or grooming the anemone depending on your point of view.

The most frequently seen and hardiest of the anemonefish is *Amphiprion percula*. It is from this species, with its stripes and wagging swimming motion, that the name clownfish was first attached to this genus. Both *A. ephippium* and *A. melanopus* are sometimes referred to as the "tomato clownfish." Both are reddish-orange with a single white stripe through the eye. *Amphiprion melanopus*, however, is darker than *A. ephippium* in certain areas, particularly the anal fin area. Several species are known as a "skunk clown" because of a white stripe running horizontally down their backs.

The anemonefishes are excellent for the aquarium although certain species are delicate when first being acclimated. During this period special care should be taken with them. Once acclimated, anemonefishes will live for a long time and enjoy a wide variety of foods, including freshly hatched brine shrimp, adult brine shrimp, and dry food.

Members of the genus *Dascyllus* are among the hardiest of marine tropicals. In their natural habitat they congregate around rocks and coral heads in numbers ranging from a handful to several hundred. They swim in unison and quickly scurry into the coral for protection at the sight of a predator. *Dascyllus* are eager eaters and will gulp down most anything from brine shrimp to dry foods. They should not be placed with more fussy eaters as the *Dascyllus* might not leave any food for them. *Dascyllus* grow very fast and should be purchased small in size so that they do not harm other members of one's aquarium. It is also best to purchase them in groups of three or more. If only a pair is

Dascyllus marginatus, family Pomacentridae. This species is very hardy, but aggressive towards other fishes. Photo by Wilhelm Hoppe.

purchased, one will become the boss and will bully the other mercilessly.

The three-spot dascyllus (*Dascyllus trimaculatus*) is all black except for a white spot on its forehead and one below its posterior dorsal fin on each side of its body. The black-and-white dascyllus (*D. aruanus*) and the black-tail dascyllus (*D. melanurus*) are both vertically striped black and white, but can be easily distinguished from one another by the black tail of *D. melanurus*.

An Atlantic species of the genus *Abudefduf* is the sergeant major (*Abudefduf saxatilis*). Perhaps the most frequently seen of the reef fishes, the sergeant major makes an excellent fish for a beginner's marine aquarium. If the sergeant major becomes dark in coloration it is a sign that the water in the aquarium is toxic or going bad, and the hobbyist should take steps to remedy the situation. Two colorful Pacific species are the Fiji blue devil (*Abudefduf uniocellatus*) and the blue devil (*A. coeruleus*). The

Pomacentrus fuscus (Juvenile), orange-backed demoiselle: Photo by Dr. Herbert R. Axelrod.

Chromis caeruleus, blue-green chromis: Photo by Dr. Herbert R. Axelrod.

Pomacentrus planifrons, orange demoiselle: Photo by Douglas Faulkner.

Equetus lanceolatus, jackknife fish: Photo by Karl Probst.

Fiji blue devil is blue with a yellow belly and tiny yellow spots throughout parts of the blue pattern. The blue devil is entirely an electric blue.

Members of the genus *Pomacentrus** include several species from the Florida Caribbean area. These species, sometimes referred to as gregories, are all similar in body shape, and tend to lose their brilliance as they grow older and larger. They usually live singularly and can only be successfully mixed in the aquarium if they are all introduced at the same time and are one inch or less in size. The beau gregory (*Pomacentrus leucostictus*) is yellow with a blue forehead or topknot. The orange damselfish (*P. planifrons*) is a bright orange species from the outer Florida reefs and the Bahamas. The flameback damselfish (*P. fuscus*) is gray with a reddish topknot. The honey gregory (*Pomacentrus* species) is a yellow orange with a purplish topknot.

A deeper-water genus of the family Pomacentridae is the *Chromis* genus, or reef fishes. The blue reef fish or blue chromis (*Chromis cyanea*), is an incandescent blue when in good health. They can be seen when one is swimming on the surface of the water even though they are fifty feet below. From the Pacific comes the blue-green chromis (*C. caeruleus*). Both of these fishes swim in large schools and more than one can be kept in an aquarium. Sizes under three inches are best. They are rather fragile and often develop fungus when first caught or moved. The fungus should be treated with a copper sulfate solution and the fins will grow back quickly.

With the exception of the anemonefish and *Chromis* species, many aquarists tend to consider the members of the Pomacentridae family as not good aquarium fish because of their aggressiveness. They are, however, relatively inexpensive, hardy, and colorful. The secret to enjoying these fishes is to carefully plan the aquarium

---

*The 1970 Edition of *A List of Common and Scientific Names of Fishes from the United States and Canada,* published by the American Fisheries Society, changes the generic name of *Eupomacentrus* to *Pomacentrus*. Since this list, which is published every ten years, is the most widely accepted and used source of identification, the genus *Pomacentrus* is used in this book. It should be noted, however, that most other books and references currently list these species as *Eupomacentrus*.

in which you are going to keep them. Timid species should not be placed with them, and plenty of shelter should be included in which they can hide.

Highhat and Jackknives
(Family—Sciaenidae)

Members of this family (Sciaenidae) that are usually kept in the marine aquarium come from the genus *Equetus*. They include the highhat (*Equetus acuminatus*), the jackknife fish (*E. lanceolatus*), and the spotted jackknife fish (*E. punctatus*). These fish are similar in that they all possess an elongated anterior dorsal fin. Young specimens have a particularly elongated dorsal fin which shortens as they mature.

These fish are rather fragile to ship and transport, but once acclimated they do quite well in the aquarium. They should not be kept with species that might nip at their fins. They require live foods such as adult brine shrimp, grass shrimp, and baby guppies their first days in captivity. After a few weeks they will accept frozen brine shrimp, although live foods should constitute the main portion of their diet. Highhats will accept dry food.

The highhat is by far the most common of the three and relatively inexpensive. The young of the highhat exhibit more stripes than either the jackknife or spotted jackknife. The young of the jackknife are a dirty white or cream color, while the young of the spotted jackknife are a clean white.

The 1970 edition of "A List of Common and Scientific Names of Fishes from the United States and Canada," published by the American Fisheries Society, lists separate species for the highhat and cubbyu. The highhat is listed as *Equetus acuminatus* while the cubbyu is *Equetus umbrosus*. Personal communication with Mr. George Miller, of the National Oceanic and Atmospheric Administration, upon whose recommendation the separation of species was made, pointed up several differences between the two species.

The prejuvenile stage of the highhat has a connecting band on top of its head between its eyes, while the prejuvenile cubbyu lacks this inter-orbital stripe.

With adults the two species can be distinguished by the width of their horizontal stripes. The highhat has seven broad dark stripes on a gray background while the cubbyu has seven narrow

Bodianus pulchellus, spotfin hogfish, Cuban hogfish: Photo by Charles Beck.

Bodianus rufus, Spanish hogfish: Photo by Karl Probst.

Labroides dimidiatus, a "cleaner" wrasse that picks parasites from other fishes, as shown here: Photo by G. Marcuse.

Coris gaimard, yellow-tail wrasse; shown in adult phase: Photo by U. Erich Friese.

dark stripes alternating with seven narrower dark stripes. It was also revealed that a shift in genera was planned from *Equetus* to *Pareques*.

Since this list, which is published every ten years, is the most widely accepted source of new identifications, this explanation has been included. It should be noted, however, that there is obviously little difference in the viability of either of these species since they were considered as one for many years by hobbyists and scientists alike.

Wrasses (Family—Labridae)

The wrasses (family Labridae) comprise a family of approximately six hundred species of fishes found throughout the tropical oceans of the world. The exact number of species is uncertain due to the fact that the young are usually colored differently from the adults, and that males and females often have different color patterns.

Wrasses are carnivorous and therefore do well on a diet of brine shrimp, cut-up shrimp, fish, and other items for variety. They are not fussy eaters, and the hogfishes in particular have lived for several years in captivity. It is best to purchase small specimens as larger specimens require a rather large swimming area and may be aggressive to other tank inhabitants. Most of the smaller wrasses bury themselves in the sand at night, and their aquarium should be equipped with a medium-coarse sand to allow them this protection. Sea anemones are best left out of an aquarium with wrasses as it could be fatal for the wrasse should it come up out of the sand under the tentacles of an anemone.

From the Florida Caribbean area come the Spanish hogfish (*Bodianus rufus*) and the spotfin or Cuban hogfish (*B. pulchellus*). The spotfin hogfish is a deep-water species usually found in over seventy-five feet of water. This, combined with the fact that they are very fast swimmers, accounts for their higher price tag. The young of the spotfin hogfish are all yellow and gradually reach adult coloration at four inches. Two wrasses often found in the home marine aquarium are the orange neon wrasse and the iridio wrasse. These are really juvenile stages of the yellowhead wrasse (*Halichoeres garnoti*) and the pudding wife wrasse (*H. radiatus*) respectively.

This adult male bluehead wrasse *(Thalassoma bifasciatum)* has a completely different color pattern from the juveniles and females. Photo by G. Marcuse.

The yellow tail wrasse *(Coris gaimardi)* is from the Pacific area, and in the juvenile stage it is an orangish red with five white spots circled in black. Also in the Pacific are the wrasses of the genus *Labroides*. These wrasses are known for their ability to remove parasites from larger fish such as groupers, snappers, and moray eels. These fish could easily swallow these little wrasses, but permit them to swim around and patiently pick at any parasites infecting the larger fish.

Scorpionfishes (Family—Scorpaenidae)

The scorpionfishes (Scorpaenidae) include many species which are capable of transmitting poison into other fishes and human beings through their hollow spines. The sacs containing the poison are located at the base of the spines. The most poisonous of this family is the stonefish *(Synanceja verrucosa)* which can cause death to a person in a few hours. This fish is seldom seen in the marine aquarium except in the large public aquariums. It is not recommended for the beginner.

Gramma loreto, royal gramma, family Grammidae. One of the best. Colorful, hardy, and relatively inexpensive—an excellent investment. Photo by Dr. Herbert R. Axelrod.

Hippocampus ·species, seahorse: Photo by H. Hansen, Aquarium Berlin.

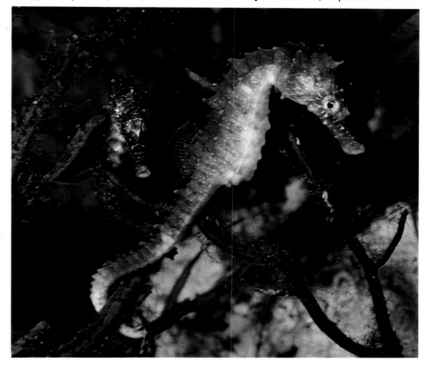

Pterois volitans, lionfish: Photo by Dr. Herbert R. Axelrod.

Pterois sphex, Hawaiian lionfish: Photo by Dr. Herbert R. Axelrod

The lionfish (*Pterois volitans*) is the most popular species within this family with marine aquarists. Although it is not as deadly as the stonefish, the lionfish can still inflict an agonizing wound, and should be handled with extreme care. The lionfish will arch its back and project its dorsal fins toward any danger. The lionfish's venom will enter the aggressor once contact has been made with the fins. Although there are no recorded deaths from lionfish venom, several poeple have ended up in a hospital as a result of receiving the venom. From Hawaii comes a somewhat less attractive lionfish (*P. sphex*) but still an interesting addition to a marine aquarium.

Lionfish have proved to be very hardy in the marine aquarium, and some have lived three or four years. They grow very quickly, and because of this it is not necessary to purchase a large specimen. Simply feed a small specimen well and one will soon have a large specimen. Freshly caught specimens will eat only live fish or shrimp, but soon can be taught to eat cut-up fish and shrimp. Once anyone has seen a lionfish "inhale" a guppy, he will realize that it would be foolish to try and keep fish much smaller than the lionfish with it.

Lionfish will spend much of their time simply lying around on the coral. This is the natural manner of this family whose fin structure serves as camouflage in the sea where they rest under ledges and on rocks and other objects near the bottom.

Seahorses (Family—Syngnathidae)

No book about marine aquariums would be complete without mentioning the ever-popular seahorse. This interesting little fish is very hardy provided the proper conditions are maintained. First of all, seahorses should be kept by themselves since they are slow eaters and other more aggressive specimens might devour all the food before the seahorse caught his fill. Secondly, most seahorses will eat only live food in the form of baby guppies, seaweed shrimp, or adult brine shrimp. Occasionally they can be trained to eat frozen brine shrimp that is circulating around the tank, but these cases are few and far between. Unless one has a steady source of live adult brine shrimp, he should not attempt to keep the large seahorses (*Hippocampus hudsonius*). Seahorses can be kept in standard goldfish bowls using the small round subsand filters

Very popular in marine aquaria is *Dendrochirus zebra*, the zebra lion fish, from the Tropical Indo-Pacific. Photo by Gerhard Budich.

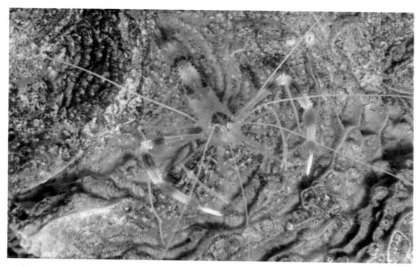

Stenopus hispidus, banded coral shrimp. These shrimp should be kept singly or in "mated" pairs to avoid fighting. Photo by Douglas Faulkner.

Colorful tropical shrimp. Many species of marine shrimps are available to hobbyists; most are very hardy. Photo by Douglas Faulkner.

Squilla mantis, mantis shrimp, fun to watch but dangerous to fish (and fingers). Photo courtesy of Alimenta—Brussels.

The shame-faced crabs (*Calappa*, etc.) are so-called because they have large claws which all but hide the face from view. Photo by Douglas Faulkner.

especially designed for them, but regularly equipped marine tanks are of course best.

The large seahorses grow to about five inches. Dwarf seahorses (*H. zosterae*) grow only to about an inch and a half. They feed mostly on baby brine shrimp in the aquarium and are miniatures of the large seahorses.

Swimming is accomplished by the seahorse using his dorsal fin, which vibrates, and through the use of tiny pectoral fins which look like ears. The seahorse can be sexed by the pouch of the male located just below its stomach. Female seahorses lack this pouch. The male seahorse has the distinction of giving birth to the baby seahorses several weeks after the female has deposited eggs in his pouch. The number of babies born at one time may reach several hundred. Anyone attempting to raise baby seahorses should have a rather large supply of baby brine shrimp on hand as this food should constantly be in the water with the babies.

Fairy Basslets (Family—Grammidae)

The fairy basslet *Gramma loreto*, or royal gramma as it is called by marine aquarists, is probably the best buy in the long line of salt water fishes. Few species, if any, can match its vivid colors and hardiness. Once a seldom-seen rarity, the royal gramma is now usually available from reputable dealers at a price most marine aquarists can afford.

The royal gramma is easily identified by its striking beauty, an anterior of vivid purple and a posterior of bright orange plus a black dot at the top of its anterior dorsal fin. A thin black line through its eye creates a mascara-like effect. Reaching a maximum of three or four inches in length, royals are therefore not as confined in an aquarium as a large angelfish. Its relatively small size at maturity makes it a likely prospect to be one of the few marine fishes whose adult stage is small enough to allow the fish to be bred in captivity.

The royal gramma is a hearty carnivorous eater. Small grass shrimp, baby guppies and live or frozen brine shrimp are all relished by royals. Dry foods are also accepted once the fish have become acclimated to their tank. The royal gramma is an exception to the rule of tailoring a fish's meals to its mouth. Although they have relatively large mouths for their body size, they feed primarily on the microscopic zooplankton which float by their underwater homes. Consequently, live baby brine shrimp should be fed frequently to this species.

Royal grammas make excellent "tankmates." They do not fight with other species and are fairly well able to protect themselves from aggressors. More than one royal can be placed in the same aquarium, but care should be taken to be sure that hiding places are available. Atlantic lettuce coral and cracked conch shells are favorite retreats.

The royal gramma is found in water from a few feet to 200 feet in Bermuda, the West Indies, and the western Caribbean. It is especially common in the Bahama Islands, where they are found swimming around coral heads and under large ledges. A peculiarity of the royal gramma is that it swims upside down under ledges but quickly "rights" itself when chased out from underneath.

The blackcap basslet, *Gramma melacara*, or imperial gramma, is a deep-water relative of the royal gramma. It is most common on drop-offs of 150 feet. Consequently it is not seen very often in marine aquariums.

Other Fishes

Although we have discussed in preceding sections many of the fishes of a number of different families that are important in the marine hobby, what we've discussed is by no means exclusive: there are many other families of fishes having representation in marine waters, and there are many species in addition to the ones we've talked about that make good specimens for marine tanks.

In choosing your fishes, remember that regardless of how attractive or interesting a fish may be and regardless of its appeal to you as a candidate for your tanks, you're not being fair to either the fish or yourself if you purchase a specimen and are unprepared to give it the special consideration its good maintenance might require. Before you buy any fish, try to learn something about its habits and needs.

Mollusks, like the flame-shell scallops shown above, can be kept in marine aquaria with special care. Cuttle fish (below) and squids are extremely difficult for experts to maintain—even for limited periods of time. Upper photo by Dr. Herbert R. Axelrod. Lower photo by H. Hansen, Aquarium Berlin.

Echinoderms, such as the sea urchin at the right and the tropical starfish shown below, often can be purchased and make excellent additions to a marine tank. Most are easy to maintain since they do not often suffer from parasites and disease. (Right) photo by Holzhammer. (Below) photo by V. D. Nieuwenhuizen.

Invertebrates

A most interesting and fascinating undertaking for the marine aquarist is an invertebrate aquarium. For such a project the hobbyist can choose among hundreds of species, from some which are very hardy to some that have never been kept successfully for any prolonged period of time.

It is preferable to keep a separate tank of invertebrates for several reasons. First of all, most marine remedies are toxic to invertebrates. If fish and invertebrates are mixed, the fish must be removed when it is necessary to treat the fish for any ailment. Also, certain crustaceans are very fragile after molting (shedding their shells) and are vulnerable to attack from their tankmates. The aquarist should be careful not to put invertebrates in aquariums that have been treated with various medicines. Some invertebrates can be lost due to chemicals remaining in the water, even after a period of several weeks. All in all, it is easier to keep them in a separate tank and not have all the extra trouble and losses.

Mentioned earlier was the sea anemone in which the anemonefish live. These are fascinating flowerlike animals. They should be fed pieces of cut-up shrimp or fish several times a week. When purchasing an anemone, check to see that its base is not torn or damaged. Anemones cling to rocks and sometimes are damaged by collectors when removing them from their location. Dead anemones quickly foul aquarium water, consequently the aquarium should be checked daily to see that the anemones are alive.

Two crustaceans often found in the marine aquarium are the banded coral shrimp (*Stenopus hispidus*) and the arrow or spider crab (*Stenorynchus seticornis*). These are two inexpensive additions which will provide the hobbyist with hours of enjoyment. They both will shed their shells, leaving behind what appears to be another shrimp or crab. If a claw or leg is broken off, it usually will regrow to its original size after several molts.

Hermit crabs are an interesting addition to a marine aquarium. These crustaceans come in a variety of colors and range in size from less than an inch to as large as a foot or more. They are excellent scavengers, and can constantly be seen searching the rocks and coral for bits of uneaten food. The shells, which are used to house and protect their tender, vulnerable "bottoms" are not of their own making, but rather are from other animals. Hermit crabs will claim the empty shell of various mollusks for their own. As the hermit crab grows, he is continually "trading-in" his current shell for a new and larger model. Consequently, the marine aquarist should place several empty shells in the hermit crab's tank for him to use as the need arises.

Sea urchins and starfish are occasionally seen in home marine aquariums. These echinoderms are fascinating to watch because of the hundreds of tubular feet which propel them around their environment. These feet, as well as the animal's mouth, can be clearly observed as they move across the aquarium's glass front. Both sea urchins and starfish will eat small bits of cut-up fish, but do not fare well over long periods of time on this type of diet. Starfish prefer live clams or oysters.

The keeping of living coral in a closed-system marine aquarium presents a tremendous challenge to the hobbyist. First of all it is difficult to obtain healthy coral specimens. A particular coral cluster should be "clean" in the sense that there is not a film encompassing it. Such a film means that the polyps have died and are decaying. It is not necessary for the polyps' tentacles to be fully extended, as most corals are nocturnal, and therefore do not open up fully until evening.

A major obstacle to keeping live coral is providing it with the necessary food. The feeding problem should be approached from the viewpoint that each polyp is a miniature sea anemone, which it is, for all practical purposes. The hobbyist should concentrate on creating conditions that will enable each polyp to feed. Depending on the size of the polyps, they will eat either freshly hatched or adult brine shrimp. The polyps will capture and devour the brine shrimp.

Most reef fish will pick on and nibble live coral, devouring individual polyps. This practice eventually results in the death of the coral. Therefore, most fishes (angelfishes in particular) should not be kept with living coral. Seahorses and certain carnivorous species, such as cardinalfishes and royal grammas, may be successfully mixed in an aquarium containing live coral.

Condylactis passiflora, with purple-tipped tentacles, is often available.
Photo by U. Erich Friese.

Oulactis muscosa has numerous tentacles set along the rim of the disc.
Photo by U. Erich Friese.

The stalk may be as colorful or even more colorful than the tentacle, as in *Tealia columbiana*. Photo by U. Erich Friese.

STARTING
A MARINE
AQUARIUM

POISONOUS
MARINE
ANIMALS

FINDLAY E. RUSSELL

This book serves a very important need for every marine aquarist, dealer and hobbyist. Primarily it deals with how marine fishes poison people (and other fishes) that handle them, eat them, disturb them or step on them! It describes in detail the kinds of poisons, which fishes are poisonous and why they are poisonous. It gives hints as to how to treat a person stung by a poisonous fish, for example, as well as how NOT to get stung! It warns about keeping certain fishes in aquariums since they can poison their tankmates . . . and it warns against eating certain very poisonous fishes, such as puffers. This new edition contains some interesting color photographs.

Published by
T.F.H. PUBLICATIONS, Inc.,
Box 27, Neptune, N.J. 07753